John
An Eyewitness Account of the Son of God

WHITNEY T. KUNIHOLM

FISHERMAN
BIBLE STUDYGUIDES

John
PUBLISHED BY WATERBROOK PRESS
12265 Oracle Boulevard, Suite 200
Colorado Springs, Colorado 80921
A division of Random House, Inc.

Unless otherwise indicated, all Scripture quotations are taken from the *Holy Bible: New International Version®*. NIV® Copyright © 1973, 1978, 1984 by International Bible Society. Used by permission of Zondervan Publishing House. All rights reserved.

10 Digit ISBN: 0-87788-429-3
13 Digit ISBN: 978-0-87788-429-3

Printed in the United States of America

2008

10   9   8   7   6   5   4

Contents

How to Use This Studyguide v
Introduction 1

1   The Living Word 3
     John 1:1-34

2   Come and See 7
     John 1:35–2:25

3   New Life 11
     John 3

4   Living Water 15
     John 4:1-42

5   Skepticism and Faith 19
     John 4:43–5:47

6   Bread of Life 23
     John 6

7   Who Is This Jesus? 29
     John 7

8   Sin and Forgiveness 35
     John 8:1-30

9   God's True Children 39
     John 8:31-59

10   Light in the Darkness 43
     John 9

11   The Good Shepherd and His Sheep 47
     John 10

12   Life and Death 51
     John 11

13 Perfume and Praise 55
    John 12

14 The Last Supper 61
    John 13

15 Comfort and Challenge 65
    John 14

16 Vines, Branches, and Fruit 69
    John 15:1–16:4

17 Peace in a Troubled World 73
    John 16:5-33

18 Jesus's Farewell Prayer 77
    John 17

19 On Trial 81
    John 18:1-27

20 Sentenced to Die 85
    John 18:28–19:16

21 The Cross 89
    John 19:17-42

22 The Empty Tomb 93
    John 20

23 A Call to Discipleship 97
    John 21

Leader's Notes 101

How to Use This Studyguide

*F*isherman studyguides are based on the inductive approach to Bible study. Inductive study is discovery study; we discover what the Bible says as we ask questions about its content and search for answers. This is quite different from the process in which a teacher *tells* a group *about* the Bible—what it means and what to do about it. In inductive study, God speaks directly to each of us through his Word.

A group functions best when a leader keeps the discussion on target, but the leader is neither the teacher nor the "answer person." A leader's responsibility is to *ask*—not *tell*. The answers come from the text itself as group members examine, discuss, and think together about the passage.

There are four kinds of questions in each study. The first is an *approach question*. Asked and answered before the Bible passage is read, this question breaks the ice and helps you start thinking about the topic of the Bible study. It begins to reveal where thoughts and feelings need to be transformed by Scripture.

Some of the earlier questions in each study are *observation questions*—who, what, where, when, and how—designed to help you learn some basic facts about the passage of Scripture.

Once you know what the Bible says, you need to ask, *What does it mean?* These *interpretation questions* help you discover the writer's basic message.

Next come *application questions,* which ask, *What does it mean to me?* They challenge you to live out the Scripture's life-transforming message.

Fisherman studyguides provide spaces between questions for jotting down responses as well as any related questions you would like to raise in the group. Each group member should have a copy of the studyguide and may take a turn in leading the group.

A group should use any accurate, modern translation of the Bible such as the *New International Version,* the *New American Standard Bible,* the *New Living Translation,* the *New Revised Standard Version,* the *New Jerusalem Bible,* or the *Good News Bible.* (Other translations or paraphrases of the Bible may be referred to when additional help is needed.) Bible commentaries should not be brought to a Bible study because they tend to dampen discussion and keep people from thinking for themselves.

SUGGESTIONS FOR GROUP LEADERS

1. Thoroughly read and study the Bible passage before the meeting. Get a firm grasp on its themes and begin applying its teachings for yourself. Pray that the Holy Spirit will "guide you into all truth" (John 16:13) so that your leadership will guide others.

2. If any of the studyguide's questions seem ambiguous or unnatural to you, rephrase them, feeling free to add others that seem necessary to bring out the meaning of a verse.

3. Begin (and end) the study promptly. Start by asking someone to pray that every participant will both understand the passage and be open to its transforming power. Remember, the Holy Spirit is the teacher, not you!

4. Ask for volunteers to read the passages aloud.

5. As you ask the studyguide's questions in sequence, encourage everyone to participate in the discussion. If some are silent, try gently suggesting, "Let's have an answer from someone who hasn't spoken up yet."

6. If a question comes up that you can't answer, don't be afraid to admit that you're baffled. Assign the topic as a research project for someone to report on next week, or say, "I'll do some studying and let you know what I find out."

7. Keep the discussion moving, but be sure it stays focused. Though a certain number of tangents are inevitable, you'll want to quickly bring the discussion back to the topic at hand. Also, learn to pace the discussion so that you finish the lesson in the time allotted.

8. Don't be afraid of silences; some questions take time to answer, and some people need time to gather courage to speak. If silence persists, rephrase your question, but resist the temptation to answer it yourself.

9. If someone comes up with an answer that is clearly illogical or unbiblical, ask for further clarification: "What verse suggests that to you?"

10. Discourage overuse of cross references. Learn all you can from the passage at hand, while selectively incorporating a few important references suggested in the studyguide.

11. Some questions are marked with a ◐. This indicates that further information is available in the Leader's Notes at the back of the guide.

12. For more information on getting a new Bible study group started and keeping it functioning effectively, read *You Can Start a Bible Study Group* by Gladys M. Hunt and *Pilgrims in Progress: Growing Through Groups* by Jim and Carol Plueddemann. (Both books are available from Shaw Books.)

Suggestions for Group Members

1. Learn and apply the following ground rules for effective Bible study. (If new members join the group later, review these guidelines with the whole group.)
2. Remember that your goal is to learn all you can *from the Bible passage being studied.* Let it speak for itself without using Bible commentaries or other Bible passages. There is more than enough in each assigned passage to keep your group productively occupied for one session. Sticking to the passage saves the group from insecurity ("I don't have the right reference books—or the time to read anything else.") and confusion ("Where did *that* come from? I thought we were studying _____.").
3. Avoid the temptation to bring up those fascinating tangents that don't really grow out of the passage you are discussing. If the topic is of common interest, you can bring it up later in informal conversation after the study. Meanwhile, help one another stick to the subject.
4. Encourage one another to participate. People remember best what they discover and verbalize for

themselves. Some people are naturally shy, while others may be afraid of making a mistake. If your discussion is free and friendly and you show real interest in what other group members think and feel, the quieter ones will be more likely to speak up. Remember, the more people involved in a discussion, the richer it will be.

5. Guard yourself from answering too many questions or talking too much. Give others a chance to share their ideas. If you are one who participates easily, discipline yourself by counting to ten before you open your mouth.

6. Make personal, honest applications and commit yourself to letting God's Word change you.

Introduction

I magine what it must have been like for the apostle John as he sat down to write his gospel. The year is around AD 90, and he is living in the busy, pagan seaport town of Ephesus. He is tired and old—maybe eighty or ninety years old—and he knows he will die soon.

Before John begins writing, though, he crosses the hard earth floor of the room and stands at the doorway, staring out into the hectic street. He is thinking back to the days when Jesus was on earth. *It all happened so fast,* John thinks, shaking his head. *Just three and a half years.* He recalls how the crowds first flocked to see this unknown sensation from Nazareth, and he still shivers to think about Jesus's first few miracles. He remembers his fear and dislike of the Pharisees, his amazement at Jesus's teaching, and his confusion in that final, frantic week. Then two memories emerge that overpower the rest: He remembers standing helplessly in the dirt beside Jesus's cross, watching him die, wondering what had gone wrong; and then he recalls seeing him alive again for the first time. *It took us so long to figure out what he had been saying all that time,* the apostle muses to himself.

Finally, John turns from the window and walks back to his empty scroll. *How can I help people understand that this man, Jesus, really is the Christ, the Son of God?* And so he begins to write: "In the beginning was the Word, and the Word was with God, and the word was God...." On and on he continues, selecting just a few of the many things Jesus said and did to write about.

God planned that John's writing would be his method of communicating with you. This studyguide is a tool for hearing the clear voice of your living God in John's gospel. The real question is, Are you ready to listen?

THE LIVING WORD

JOHN 1:1-34

*T*hroughout the centuries before Jesus came to earth, God told his children, the Israelites, what he wanted of them. He did this in the days of Moses through the words of the Ten Commandments. Then there were kings and leaders who tried to convince the people to live as God instructed them to live. And through scores of prophets, God proclaimed his Word to Israel. But in spite of so many expressions of God's Word to his people, the Israelites continually failed, unable or unwilling to live according to God's plan.

So God decided to come to Earth himself and show his creatures, in person, exactly who he was and what he desired from humankind. Jesus Christ was God on Earth, showing us more clearly than ever before what he had been saying for centuries.

That's why John began his gospel by repeating the mysterious phrase, "the Word." John realized that Jesus was the final *Word of instruction.* What God had been saying for years and years, he now made crystal clear in the life, death, and resurrection of his own Son. Jesus Christ was actually God in the flesh. He was and still is the Living Word.

1. Recall the first time you or your child recognized words and learned to read. What was this experience like?

   Wow
   unbelievable

Read John 1:1-13.

2. List the characteristics and actions of "the Word" found in these verses.

   Beginning
   Was God
   With god

3. Describe the reactions to "the Word" that John observed. By referring to Jesus Christ as "the Word," what do you suppose John was trying to tell us?

   how people didn't recognize
   him, even though he was
   God
   The Word vs. "the law"
   that the Pharisees followed

*4. According to verse 12, how does a person become a child of God?

*believe + receive
He gave us the right*

READ JOHN 1:14-28.

5. What more do you learn about Jesus, "the Word," in these verses? Explain in your own words the significance of the Word becoming flesh.

*grace + truth comes thru
Jesus Christ
gave us someone to relate
to, to go what we go thru*

6. Who was John the Baptist and how did he view his own purpose in life?

*the preparer for Jesus,
warner that he was coming
lowly compared to Jesus*

7. How does John the Baptist's attitude toward Jesus shape your own attitude toward Jesus? toward yourself?

humble humble humble

⊘ READ JOHN 1:29-34.

8. Who did John the Baptist believe Jesus was? How was John the Baptist able to identify Jesus? What was the difference between John's baptism and Jesus's (verse 26)?

Son of God

John baptizes w/ water + Jesus w/ the spirit

9. Reread verse 34. Can you make that same bold statement? Why? How can you "see" God's Living Word today?

COME AND SEE

JOHN 1:35–2:25

S ome people make the decision to follow Christ at huge crusades. Others make that choice in their own home or in an airplane or in conversation with a friend. Regardless of the setting, each person comes to Christ as an individual.

Today's passage shows that following Jesus is usually a response, either to the witness of someone who has pointed the way to Jesus or to the call of Christ himself.

1. What people in your life have helped you under-stand who Jesus is?

Aunt Sylvia
Mom & Dad
Barber   Dave Champess

READ JOHN 1:35-51.

2. List the various characters in this passage and indi-cate how each one found out about Jesus.

Andrew
Simon Peter
Phillip
Nathanel

What different reactions to Jesus do you find in these verses?

He walked past them & they followed Him – they knew without fanfare that He was the messiah.

tell 2 friends, & so on

3. What is your personal attitude toward telling others about Jesus? What do the examples of John, Andrew, and Philip teach you about witnessing for Christ?

John witnesses to 2 & then they

READ JOHN 2:1-11.

4. What does Mary's statement in verse 3 indicate about her view of Jesus, her son?

That He could take care of all things

5. What does Jesus's response indicate about his attitude toward his mother? toward his own mission in life?

Respectful but loyal to God & His timing

6. What does this miracle—creating new wine from plain water—symbolize about Jesus?

7. How did the disciples react to the miracle? How do you react? What new attitudes, habits, and desires has Jesus brought about in your life?

put their faith in Him

JOHN 2:12-25.

8. What change did Jesus make in the temple? What adjectives would you use to describe Jesus's actions?

get rid of all the market people

9. How did the disciples react to Jesus's outburst? How did the Jews react?

🖉 10. Jesus answered the Jews by referring to a new kind of temple. Why was it different from the temple the Jews had in mind?

11. Jesus could see that the livestock sellers and money changers upset true worship of God. What things detract from your time of worship? How could you improve your worship?

NEW LIFE

JOHN 3

*W*e all experience drastic changes at some point in our lives. These events drastically alter our routines and challenge the ways we have learned to cope. Maybe it's graduating from school or landing that first permanent job. Maybe it's getting married or moving to another town or state. Maybe it's having a baby or seeing our children leave home, or maybe it's the loss of someone we love.

Whatever the change, it marks a transition in our lives; a change from one way of living to a totally different way. It is an event that in some way gives us a new life.

In these next few chapters, John described the biggest and most profound change that any person could ever make: believing in Jesus Christ, the Living Word. This belief literally gives a person a new life that lasts forever.

1. What was the biggest change in your life in the last five years? How did it affect you?

READ JOHN 3:1-15.

2. Who was Nicodemus? What did he believe about Jesus?

Pharisee

felt God was with him but not Son of God - Christ

3. Jesus quickly changed the subject to the new birth. What did Jesus say about this new birth? Have you experienced the new birth? If so, how has it made a difference in your life?

Couldn't be in kingdom of heaven w/o being born again of the spirit & of water

READ JOHN 3:16-21.

4. List as many truths about the new life as you can find in verse 16.

God loved the world

gave His Son

Believing in Him u will not perish

5. Why did God send his Son into the world (verse 17)?
   How should people respond to this act (verse 18)?

   to save - not ~~condemn~~
   condemn the world
   need to believe

✗ 6. What does it mean to "come into the light" (verses
   20-21)? Explain by using examples from your own
   life. How do others see the light in your life?

   believe in Jesus, live by
   God's word
   walk the walk

7. Replace the word *world* in verses 16 and 17 with the
   name of a friend whose salvation you are praying
   for. Take time to pray silently for that friend now.

READ JOHN 3:22-36.

8. What appear to have been the most important
   concerns of John's disciples? What did John reveal
   about his own ministry by his response? What did
   he reveal about God?

   That Jesus was baptizing
   He is willing to be humble -
   Jesus is greater, John was less

9. What was the most important concern of John the Baptist (verse 30)? What are you most concerned about? What are some specific ways you could live out verse 30?

He must become greater, I must become less.

LIVING WATER

JOHN 4:1-42

*J*ohn continued to reveal who Jesus was through his encounters with various people. For John the Baptist and Nathanael, faith seemed to come easily. Faith was difficult for Nicodemus because he saw himself as a good man. He had to learn that even though he was a pious religious leader, he was condemned without the gift of new life.

Now we meet an outcast Samaritan woman. Unlike Nicodemus who had a good reputation, she was known for her immorality. Faith came hard for her because she knew she was a great sinner. Jesus drew her, step by step, until she realized that God valued her and wanted her to have eternal life and to worship him.

1. Has faith come easily for you or have you struggled to believe? Explain.

   Always believed, just not always followed.

Read John 4:1-15.

2. For what reasons would this woman have encountered prejudice in her day (verse 9)?

   Samaritan

3. What was Jesus's attitude toward her? What are some groups that encounter discrimination today? How can Jesus's example shape your attitude toward these groups?

   didn't care
   poor, ethnicities, the
   list goes on.

4. Explain how Jesus used the word *water*. Specifically, what is "living water" (verse 10)? What effect does it have in your life (verses 10,14)?

   eternal life
   to never thirst

Read John 4:16-26.

5. What was this Samaritan woman's sin? How did Jesus find out? What does this teach you about "secret sins"?

   There R no certain
   sins.

6. What did Jesus reveal about the "new worship" he
   was introducing? What did he mean by worship
   that is "in spirit" and "in truth"?

*worship in spirit &
truth - relational vs.
geographical (radical)*

7. What does Jesus's encounter with this woman teach
   you about approaching others with the message of
   the gospel?

*Anybody & everybody
should hear about it.
not to worry how crazy it
sounds.*

READ JOHN 4:27-42.

8. What kinds of prejudice might the disciples have had
   toward others? How was Jesus's attitude different?

*Same as others of
that time- and*

9. What secret did Jesus reveal to the Samaritan
   woman (verse 26)? What did it motivate her to
   do (verses 28-29)?

*That He was the Messiah.
Tell every one in the
town.*

10. What was Jesus's most important concern (verse 34)? Give an example of how you could make this the greatest concern in your daily life.

> *Do the will of him who sent me.*

11. Explain what the following terms have to do with sharing the new life with others:

fields (verse 35)

> *don't wait til everything is "ripe" – do it now*

harvest (verse 35)

wages (verse 36)

12. What two factors caused the Samaritans from the woman's village to accept the new life Jesus offered (verses 39,42)? How do these factors encourage you as you tell others about Jesus?

> *Her excited testimony & Jesus' word*

SKEPTICISM AND FAITH

JOHN 4:43–5:47

*I*sn't it amazing how two people can look at the exact same events and come up with completely opposite opinions? Two scientists examine the data of the natural world. One will remark, "Nature clearly demonstrates God's love for and control of the universe. The more I study living things, the more I stand in awe of God's genius in creation."

But miles away in a different lab, another scientist concludes, "I see no evidence of any 'mind' or order behind the myriad empirical facts. In nature there is order, but there is also chaos. There are devastating earthquakes as well as beautiful butterflies. Who can be sure there is an underlying purpose?"

In the next section of John's gospel, Jesus performed some astounding miracles. How did the people who saw these things respond? You will see an amazing blend of belief and unbelief. As you watch this interplay of skepticism and faith, ask yourself, What preconceived ideas have I latched on to? Take the risk of coming to your studies with the same attitude as the psalmist of old who cried, "Search me, O God, and know my heart; test me and know my anxious thoughts. See if there is any offensive way in me, and lead me in the way everlasting" (Psalm 139:23-24).

1. Recall a time when someone in your family was seriously ill. How did the family cope with this illness?

READ JOHN 4:43-54.

2. In what ways did the official demonstrate faith in Jesus (verses 47,50,53)?

3. John noted that this healing was Jesus's "second miraculous sign" in Galilee (verse 54). What does the healing teach you about Jesus?

Jesus knew they would not believe w/out seeing many miracles—

READ JOHN 5:1-15.

4. Summarize the sick man's encounter with Jesus. Did he seem to exhibit faith and/or skepticism regarding Jesus? In what way?

Both—
didn't know it was Jesus, was just trying to get to healing water

5. How did the Jews react to Jesus's healing of the sick man? What specific complaints did they have against Jesus?

That he picked up his mat on the sabbath

6. What do Jesus's actions in this incident teach you about God's concern for those "paralyzed by sin"?

asked if he wanted to get well, told him to get up

no matter how paralyzed by sin we r he can make us whole

7. Can you think of situations in your own church or fellowship where people seem to resist the living presence of Jesus in favor of customs, habits, or traditions? How should you handle such situations?

Older traditions

Read John 5:16-30.

8. What facts did Jesus reveal about his relationship with the Father? How would these facts have answered his skeptics' complaints (verse 18)?

compared his relationship w/ father - Son strived w/ that

Said He was doing what the Father told Him & they wanted to kill him more

9. What future event did Jesus describe? What details about this event does he give us? Why do you suppose he said these things to that particular audience?

Judgement given by the Father for eternal life — said to a judgemental crowd

10. What reassuring truth do you find in verse 24? Explain what Jesus meant by "hears" and "believes." What specific claim was Jesus defending in these verses?

Hearing + believing by living out Jesus' words to claim eternal life — Faith

READ JOHN 5:31-47.

11. List all the "witnesses" Jesus offered his skeptics as proof of his claims about his relationship with God.

*John
moses*

12. How did Jesus characterize these Jews? What mistake had the Jews made in their study of the Scriptures (verses 39-40,46)? What principle do you find here for your own Bible study?

BREAD OF LIFE

JOHN 6

*P*eople today argue about Jesus's identity just as they did when he was on earth. Was he merely a good teacher or was he really God? The Jews of Jesus's day wanted him to be their political savior, to lead them against the Romans. When he provided free food for five thousand, they were sure he was their Messiah. But when he quietly withdrew from the clamoring crowds, they were puzzled. Jesus's disciples were still trying to figure him out too. He could multiply loaves of bread, yet he claimed that physical food was of relative unimportance. Then he called *himself* bread. What could he mean by that?

1. How long does it take for you to feel physical hunger? Do you have similar longings for God's presence? Explain.

    Unfortunately) not –

READ JOHN 6:1-15.

2. Why did the crowd follow Jesus?

Saw miraculous signs he performed on the sick

3. Why did Jesus ask Philip what to do about feeding all the people? What did Philip's answer indicate about his own faith in Jesus? What about Andrew's statement?

to test him

they didn't trust Jesus, Saw all those miracles & still turned to $ & themselves

4. After Jesus fed the multitude, what did they want to do to him? How did Jesus react to this?

they wanted to force him to be king & so he withdrew

READ JOHN 6:16-21.

5. How should Jesus's feeding of the five thousand have helped the disciples during the storm crisis? What did they still need to learn?

Knew he just performed miracle of feeding - still didn't trust & were frightened.

6. Compare verses 16-21 to Matthew 14:22-33.
   What additional information did Matthew report
   on this incident? What do Peter's words and actions
   (Matthew 14:28-31) indicate about his faith?

   Peter still tested him,
   & was still afraid when
   there was wind- took
   eyes off Jesus & "saw danger"

READ JOHN 6:22-40.

7. The crowd, still confused about who Jesus was,
   came "in search of Jesus." According to Jesus's statement in verse 26, what is often the motive behind
   our seeking him?

   to be "filled" - what
   we long for

8. How did Jesus define "the work of God"?

   to believe the one He
   sent

9. What did Jesus mean by calling himself "the bread
   of life"?

   total fulfillment with
   belief in him

10. What facts about salvation do you notice in verses 37-40?

He is sent to do God's will & not lose one of us that believes in him

READ JOHN 6:41-51.

11. Why were the Jews skeptical about Jesus's claims concerning himself?

They knew he'd been "born" and they knew his parents

12. Verse 44 states that the Father draws people to Jesus. How have you experienced this?

READ JOHN 6:52-71.

13. What do you think Jesus was trying to communicate by the words "eats my flesh and drinks my blood"? What would be the benefits of this eating and drinking?

totally consume remember Him Jesus nourishes you Trusting in Him

14. Describe the degrees of faith and skepticism you see in the Jews (verse 52) and "many of his disciples" (verses 60,66).

15. Why did Peter believe in Jesus (verses 67-69)? Why do you believe in Jesus?

Saw he was fulfilling prophets, took leap to believe in Him

WHO IS THIS JESUS?

JOHN 7

I magine a television reporter going back in time two thousand years to Jerusalem…

"Excuse me, sir. Could you tell our audience who the one they call Jesus is?"

"Jesus? Ah, he's that guy everybody wants to see. They say he does some pretty fancy tricks. He was giving out free food one day. I don't know who he is, but if he keeps that up, he'll have a lot of followers."

"Excuse me, Rabbi. What do you know about Jesus? Who is he?"

"He's a blasphemer and a troublemaker—thinks he's *God!* And he exhibits flagrant disregard for our Law. If he doesn't stop riling up the people, the Romans will use it as an excuse to make our lives more miserable!"

"Tell me, ma'am. Have you seen Jesus? Who do you think he is?"

"Yes, I've seen Jesus. He is the Son of God. He will save us and give us eternal life. Go see for yourself. Then you'll know who he is."

"Who is this Jesus?" If your view of Jesus's identity is still a little fuzzy, be brave enough to define your questions and make a serious attempt to answer them in these next studies.

1. Do you have family or friends who think your beliefs are foolish? How do they express this?

READ JOHN 7:1-13.

2. Where had Jesus gone? Why?

3. What advice did Jesus's brothers give him? In what sense do you think his brothers "did not believe in him" (verse 5)?

4. Identify some of the opinions about Jesus that were expressed among those at the feast. What hindered open discussion about Jesus?

READ JOHN 7:14-36.

5. Why were the Jews so amazed at Jesus? What did Jesus say about his teaching?

6. What deeper motive did Jesus perceive in the people with whom he spoke? What logic did Jesus use to show their inconsistency? (Review John 5:2-18.)

7. Summarize how the following groups were struggling with the question of Jesus's identity:

    the people of Jerusalem (verses 25-27)

    the people who believed (verse 31)

    the Pharisees and the chief priests (verse 32)

the Jews (verses 35-36)

8. How did Jesus explain who he was (verses 28-29)?
   To what future event was he referring in verses 33
   and 34?

READ JOHN 7:37-53.

9. What invitation did Jesus give on the last day of the
   feast? Explain what he meant by the words *thirst*
   and *drink*.

10. How did the confusion continue about who Jesus
    was (verses 40-47)? What reasons did people give
    for their opinions?

11. What attitude did the chief priests and Pharisees have about Jesus? Why do you think they felt this way? What did Nicodemus suggest? What caused him to say this (verses 50-51; see also 3:1-21)?

12. What opinions do people today have about Jesus's identity? What opportunities do you have to generate open discussion about who Jesus is?

Sin and Forgiveness

John 8:1-30

*J*esus continued to make astounding claims about himself—and his opponents continued to challenge him. Trying to trap him, they brought a woman to him who had been caught in the act of adultery. She was undoubtedly guilty, but she was also probably the victim of a malicious plot. The religious leaders wanted to put Jesus in an impossible situation; he would have to either oppose the law of Moses, which called for the death penalty, or the law of Rome, which forbade the death penalty in such a case. Jesus showed that his concern was for the woman—he defended her and accepted her, yet he called her action sin and told her to give it up.

1. Think of a time when you were caught in a wrongful act. How did you feel?

READ JOHN 8:1-11.

✐ 2. Why had Jesus gone to the temple? Why had the
teachers of the law and the Pharisees gone to the
temple? What does this contrast indicate about
the spiritual leaders of that time?

✐ 3. What was the woman's sin? How did the teachers of
the law and the Pharisees treat her? What obvious
hypocrisy do you notice about their accusation?

4. What do you learn about forgiveness from Jesus's
actions and words? In what situation do you need to
apply Jesus's example and teaching on forgiveness?

5. What does Jesus's assumption that he could forgive this woman reveal about his identity? Against whom had the woman sinned?

READ JOHN 8:12-20.

6. What analogy did Jesus use to explain who he was (verse 12)? What does it teach you about Jesus?

7. Why did the Pharisees consider Jesus's claim invalid? What two witnesses did Jesus offer in his defense?

READ JOHN 8:21-30.

8. What did Jesus say was going to happen in the future to him? to his listeners? How could they avoid this?

✐ 9. How did Jesus contrast himself with his listeners? How did they react? What event did Jesus say would clearly explain his identity? Now how did the listeners react?

10. How would you explain verse 24 to an unbelieving friend who is sincerely trying to live a morally good life?

GOD'S TRUE CHILDREN

JOHN 8:31-59

*T*he Jews saw themselves as free descendants of Abraham. Not so said Jesus. He called them slaves to sin and children of the devil. Strong words, but Jesus was trying to penetrate their false sense of security based on their "superior state" as Abraham's descendants. Only the truth could set them—and us—free. Whoever rejects the truth remains a slave.

1. How much do you know about your ancestors? How does that information affect the way you view yourself?

READ JOHN 8:31-47.

2. To whom was Jesus speaking in verse 31? How were they to know whether or not they were true

believers (verses 31-32)? What would be the test of this "holding to Christ's teaching" in your own life?

3. What did the Jews point to as proof of their superior spiritual state? How is it possible to make the same kind of mistake today?

4. What accusations did Jesus level at the Jews (verses 37,40,44)? What reasons did he give for these words (verses 39,42-43,45)?

5. How did Jesus sum up the basic cause of the continuing antagonism between himself and the Jews, the

teachers of the Law, and the Pharisees (verse 47)?
What ramifications does this have on your witness
for Christ today?

READ JOHN 8:48-59.

6. What bitter counteraccusation did the Jews hurl
at Jesus? To whom did Jesus refer for his defense?
What does this tell you about Jesus?

7. Explain Jesus's startling claim in verse 51. What
did he mean by "keeps my word" and "never see
death"?

8. When the Jews again interrogated Jesus about his
identity (verse 53), how did he answer? Does this
seem like a clear answer in your opinion? Why or
why not?

9. Now how did the Jews react (verse 59)? Have you ever known a person who offered bitter, vocal opposition to Christ? From this passage, what can you learn from Jesus's example about how to handle such a situation?

LIGHT IN THE DARKNESS

JOHN 9

*T*he incident in this passage brings up the age-old question of why people suffer. And it points out some interesting twists about who the blind really are.

1. What would you miss most if you couldn't see?

READ JOHN 9:1-12.

2. What was the disciples' primary interest in the blind man? What does this indicate about them?

3. What does Jesus's answer reveal about the cause of some sickness or misfortune? How could this truth be applied and misapplied today?

4. How does Jesus's statement in verse 5 explain what he did to the blind man? How was this miracle related to Jesus's continuing argument with the Jewish leaders?

5. How did the neighbors react to this miracle? What does this tell you about them?

READ JOHN 9:13-34.

6. Describe the ex-blind man's developing belief in Jesus. Explain by contrast his opinion of the Pharisees.

7. What was the attitude of the ex-blind man's parents? In what situations in your life might you be tempted to make a similar mistake?

8. Explain how the ex-blind man outwitted the Pharisees. What does their reaction reveal about them? If a person has already decided he or she does not want to believe in Jesus, is it of any value to share the gospel with that person? Why or why not?

READ JOHN 9:35-41.

9. How did the ex-blind man finally come to know Jesus's identity? How did he act on his belief?

10. How did Jesus use this occasion to further reveal his mission on earth?

11. Review this entire chapter. List the various steps toward faith this ex-blind man took (verses 11-12, 17,25,33,38). List the steps toward faith that you have taken. How might this affect your attitude and actions toward unbelievers and honest seekers?

12. Jesus condemned the Pharisees because they claimed to "see" (verses 39-41). What did he mean? When might you unwittingly make this same erroneous claim?

Pray that God will keep you from spiritual arrogance.

THE GOOD SHEPHERD AND HIS SHEEP

JOHN 10

*A*ll of us face times when we don't know where to turn or who to trust. Today's passage points to Jesus, the Good Shepherd, as our source of strength and security. The Shepherd knows his sheep and protects them. He even gives his life for them so they can experience life in all its fullness.

1. What does a typical shepherd do for his sheep?

READ JOHN 10:1-21.

2. How does this passage portray Jesus as a good shepherd?

3. What strikes you as being most significant about the shepherd's relationship to the sheep?

4. What two phrases did Jesus use to describe himself (verses 7,11,14)? What does each one teach you about Jesus?

5. What two major aspects of Jesus's mission on earth did he reveal (verses 10,15)? How are they related?

6. What qualities in your life might convince an unbeliever that you possess the full life Jesus spoke about (verse 10)? How might you experience this abundant life to a greater degree?

Read John 10:22-42.

7. In light of verse 31, do you believe the Jews honestly meant what they said in verse 24? Why or why not? What infuriated them?

8. Jesus humiliated the Jews by proving that their hard hearts were causing their ignorance about his identity. How specifically did he do this (verses 32-39)?

9. How could verses 27-30 help someone who has doubts about his or her faith?

10. Some people say that Jesus was a very good man and a great teacher, but he was not God. How can you refute this argument, using verse 30?

LIFE AND DEATH

JOHN 11

*J*esus often used physical examples to illustrate spiritual truth. In today's passage, Jesus said, "He who believes in me will live, even though he dies." Immediately after making that claim, Jesus proved its truth in the most unforgettable way. He walked to the tomb of his dead friend Lazarus and commanded him to come back to life—and he did! Some people, like the high priest Caiaphas, hated Jesus for this and planned to kill him. Others, like Mary, loved Jesus and worshiped him. What is your response?

1. When have you felt that God was late in responding to your needs?

Read John 11:1-16.

2. What kind of relationship did Jesus have with Mary, Martha, and Lazarus? What does this teach you about Jesus?

3. With what problem is Jesus presented in verse 3? What did he do about it? How did he explain the delay?

4. What came to the disciples' minds when Jesus suggested a trip to Judea (verses 8,16)? Explain Jesus's response.

5. What did Jesus say was the purpose for Lazarus's death (verse 15)? What does Thomas's comment indicate about his faith in Jesus?

READ JOHN 11:17-37.

6. What two attitudes did Martha reveal? Of what did Jesus assure her? How did she interpret this statement?

7. Answer the question at the end of verse 26 as if it were addressed to you (and it is). How did Martha answer?

8. What remedy for doubt did Jesus give Martha? What reward did he promise? How might this apply to you?

9. What emotion seems to lie behind Mary's words to Jesus? How did Jesus respond? What does this indicate to you about Jesus?

READ JOHN 11:38-44.

10. Why did Jesus pray? What hint does that give you about the purpose of the work he was about to perform? What does this miracle reveal about Jesus?

READ JOHN 11:45-57.

11. In what two ways did the Jews react to the raising of Lazarus? How did the Pharisees react to the news?

12. How did Caiaphas unwittingly become a prophet of the good effects of Jesus's coming death? How did John confirm this?

13. Why do people become afraid or even resist when God works today? What are some examples of this? How do *you* resist God's work?

PERFUME AND PRAISE

JOHN 12

*J*esus was in the final week of his life. His approaching death dominated his thoughts, yet no one else comprehended what he was facing. Mary's act of love was genuine, but the crowd's praise turned hollow. Jesus continued to teach, to perform miracles, and to bring light into the darkness.

1. What would you do if you knew you had only one week left to live?

READ JOHN 12:1-11.

2. What did Mary do for Jesus? What does this tell you about her? about her opinion of Jesus?

3. What objection did Judas make to Mary's beautiful act of devotion to Christ? Was he sincere? Why or why not (verse 6)? How does this help you understand Jesus's statement to him in verse 8?

4. How did the chief priests enlarge their evil plans (verse 10)? What drove them to such extremes?

5. How could you, like Mary, express your devotion to Christ this week? Is there something valuable (not necessarily a possession) that you could or should give up to accomplish this? What should your motive be?

READ JOHN 12:12-26.

6. What motivated the crowd's acclaim for Jesus when he entered Jerusalem? What did their name for him reveal about their expectations?

7. How did Jesus choose to enter the city? What does this demonstrate about the kind of savior Jesus is? (See Zechariah 9:9, the passage John quotes in verse 15.)

8. How does Jesus's analogy of a kernel of wheat explain what he knew would soon happen to him?

9. Explain Jesus's statement in verse 25 in your own words.

10. What does it mean for you to serve and follow Jesus (verse 26)?

READ JOHN 12:27-50.

11. How is Jesus's humanity seen in verse 27? But what was Jesus's number one priority?

12. In what two ways did the crowd react to the voice of God? How did Jesus react? What things were soon to be accomplished?

13. How would verse 36 help you talk with a person who says that he or she is not ready to make a

decision about Jesus? In what ways should your life be evidence that you are a son or daughter of the light?

14. What two responses to Jesus do you find in verses 37 and 42? How can verse 43 challenge you in terms of the priorities you set for your life?

THE LAST SUPPER

JOHN 13

*J*esus's time on earth was drawing to a close. The disciples had heard Jesus's teaching and watched his miracles. Now he demonstrated his love and humility in a powerful, unforgettable way. God's beloved Son took on the role of a slave.

1. When have you seen love demonstrated in a remarkable way?

READ JOHN 13:1-11.

2. As this supper began, what things were on Jesus's mind? What did Jesus do for the disciples? Describe

what you might have thought and felt if you had been a disciple in this scene.

3. How did Peter react to Jesus's act at first? How did his reaction change and what caused it?

4. How do Jesus's actions and words demonstrate his purpose in coming to the world? How was this purpose different from the popular view of what the Messiah would be like?

5. What are some "dangers" of humility? How does Jesus's example challenge you?

READ JOHN 13:12-20.

6. How did Jesus describe himself? How did he use this description to explain why he washed the disciples' feet? What was his point?

7. What two important aspects of following Jesus are mentioned in verse 17? Why are both important?

8. How did Jesus summarize his washing of the disciples' feet (verses 15-16)? Give a practical example of how this applies to you.

READ JOHN 13:21-38.

     9. Why was Jesus so upset? How did the disciples
interpret this? To what event was Jesus referring in
verse 31?

     10. What new command did Jesus institute (verse 34)?
Although this is not a "new" command (see Leviticus 19:18), why were the disciples to have a new
understanding of its meaning? How can Jesus's
example transform *your* understanding of "love"?

COMFORT AND CHALLENGE

JOHN 14

*J*esus comforted his disciples by assuring them that their final destination was certain and that the route was clearly known. No matter what happened in their lives, their hearts did not need to be troubled. Jesus also assured his followers that his work on earth would go on through them by the power of the Holy Spirit. The same comfort and challenge strengthens our lives today.

1. Recall a time when you were lost. What emotions did you experience?

READ JOHN 14:1-14.

2. What was Jesus talking about in verses 2-4? How
    did that relate to Peter's question (see 13:36-37)?
    Why might the disciples have been troubled? What
    do Thomas's and Philip's questions indicate about
    the spiritual understanding of the disciples?

3. How does verse 6 help you respond to someone
    who says, "Each person must discover his or her
    own way to God. There's the Christian way, the
    Jewish way, the Eastern way, and many other ways.
    It's not important which way a person chooses"?

READ JOHN 14:15-24.

4. What was Jesus's "test" for love (verses 15,21,23)?

5. About whom was Jesus talking in verses 16 and 17? What facts did he reveal about this person?

6. Describe the miraculous kind of fellowship Jesus had in mind in verse 20. Upon what is this fellowship dependent? When does it occur? What experience of this fellowship have you had?

READ JOHN 14:25-31.

⊘ 7. What special duty did Jesus say the Holy Spirit will perform? Why did the disciples need this? Why do you?

8. Why did Jesus talk about peace at this time? What kind of peace does the world offer? What kind of peace was Jesus referring to (see Philippians 4:7)?

9. What advantage did Jesus speak of when he alluded to his imminent death? How could your daily routine reflect this perspective?

10. How can the work of the Holy Spirit help you in your study of God's Word? in prayer?

VINES, BRANCHES, AND FRUIT

JOHN 15:1–16:4

*P*arents work continually to teach independence to their children. It's a gradual process, from learning to tie shoes to learning how to drive and write checks. A dad tells his son, "You need to learn to do this on your own because a day will come when I won't be with you to help you."

But Jesus taught just the opposite about our relationship with him. He wants us to learn a full dependence upon his power, wisdom, and assurance. "You can't do anything without me." And he promises that he will be with us always.

1. By nature, do you tend to be an independent "free spirit" or more of a group-oriented person?

READ JOHN 15:1-17.

2. Think for a moment about a grapevine. List as many basic facts about it as you can. How does its

life begin? What causes it to grow? What does it
need to live? What can disturb or kill it?

3. Describe how Jesus used this analogy. Who is the
   vine? Who are the branches? Who is the gardener?
   Two important parts of the analogy are "bearing
   fruit" and "remaining in me." Explain what is
   required for each to happen. Use the whole passage
   for your answer.

4. What commandment did Jesus reiterate in verses 12
   and 17? What is the supreme example of obedience
   to this command (verse 13)? In what relationship(s)

or area(s) of your life do you sense God's call to obey this command more fully?

READ JOHN 15:18–16:4.

5. What did Jesus mean when he said, "You do not belong to the world"? Because of this, what did Jesus predict about the world's reaction to Christians?

6. How does a person become aware of sin (15:22)? How does this explain the reaction of some people to Jesus?

7. In what ways and on what occasions did Jesus say the Holy Spirit would testify about him (15:26)?

8. Have you ever been hated because of Jesus? If so, when and how? Are there ways you are avoiding the "hate" of unbelievers? What should you do for Christ's sake that might cause you to be hated by your unbelieving friends?

9. Look again at all of today's passages. What resources has God given you to obey the command in 15:12?

PEACE IN A TROUBLED WORLD

JOHN 16:5-33

*J*esus predicted a difficult future for his disciples. They would face hardship, persecution, and death. But they wouldn't face those things alone. Today's passage shows why secure joy is possible even in the midst of a troubled world.

1. Describe a time when you had to say a difficult good-bye. What made it hard?

READ JOHN 16:5-15.

2. How did the disciples feel at this point? (Review Jesus's warnings to them in verses 1-4.)

3. What did Jesus say to clarify their perspective (verse 7)?

4. Explain the purpose for each of the three aspects of the Holy Spirit's work mentioned in verses 8-11.

5. What aspects of the Spirit's work did Jesus include in verses 13-15?

6. How have you experienced the teaching of the Holy Spirit? How could verse 13 encourage you?

Read John 16:16-33.

✐ 7. What bothered the disciples most about Jesus's explanations (verses 16-18)? Why do you suppose this was the case?

8. How did Jesus's analogy about a woman giving birth enhance his explanation of verse 20?

9. Is the last part of verse 23 an accurate description of your prayer life? How should your prayers reflect the union with Christ and the Spirit to which Jesus referred?

10. What is the reason you can experience genuine peace (verse 33)? Do you, in fact, experience a greater degree of peace than unbelievers you know? How could you share this peace with others?

JESUS'S FAREWELL PRAYER

JOHN 17

*W*hat does it mean to be in the world, but not of it? Jesus's farewell prayer dealt with this difficult paradox. If we adopt the lifestyle and values of the world, God is left without a witness to his grace. But if we withdraw and separate ourselves from the world, God is also left without a witness. That's why Jesus sent his disciples into the world and prayed for their protection from evil.

1. In what ways do you feel at home in this world? In what ways do you feel like an alien?

READ JOHN 17:1-19.

2. What facts about the scope of Jesus's activities and his relationship with the Father can you glean from verses 1-5? How did Jesus define the eternal life he gives?

3. Summarize Jesus's prayer for his disciples. What was his main concern? Why do you think he had this concern?

4. What did Jesus ask God to give his disciples (verse 13)? Is this quality seen in your life? How is it evident?

5. How can you experience the joy of Christ during times of sadness or depression?

 6. Explain Jesus's use of the phrase "of the world" (verses 14-16). How are you not of the world? To what evidence can you point?

READ JOHN 17:20-26.

7. About whom did Jesus pray (verse 20)? What was his concern for them?

8. How does the fact of your union with God through Christ affect your actions, words, and attitudes? How else should it affect you?

9. What is the ultimate purpose behind the unity of which Jesus spoke?

10. How could your unity be a testimony to the world?

11. What final statement of his own mission did Jesus make here? From all that you've learned in the book of John so far, how would you summarize Jesus's mission?

12. What implications does Jesus's mission have for your own purpose in life (verse 18)?

ON TRIAL

JOHN 18:1-27

*I*f you read a daily newspaper or listen to the news, you may have trouble understanding how God is working all things out according to his purposes. All things? Even the murder of innocent children? Or the assassination of public figures working for peace? Or the widespread sale and social acceptance of hard drugs? Certainly some acts are so evil, so vile, that it seems there is no way God can bring good from them. But when we study the crucifixion of Jesus, we begin to understand how God can use all things for his glory. The torturous execution of an innocent man (especially *this* man, the Son of God) is certainly representative of the evil in this world. Yet through that murder, God accomplished the salvation of humankind.

1. How do you typically react to the daily news stories you hear or see? With detachment? Apathy? Despair?

READ JOHN 18:1-11.

2. What action did Judas take? What does the mention of "weapons" (verse 3) indicate about Judas's expectations about the encounter? But how did Jesus react?

3. What curious occurrence took place in verse 6? How do you interpret this? What specifically happened? What truth about Jesus might John have been emphasizing?

4. How did Peter try to handle the tense situation? What does this reveal about his understanding and trust in Jesus? How did Jesus respond to Peter's act?

5. What tense situations are you facing right now? How are you tempted to take matters into your own hands? What would it mean for you to trust Jesus completely in these matters?

READ JOHN 18:12-27.

6. Trace Peter's actions in these verses. What do you think motivated his repeated denials? What is significant about Peter's attitude here (review John 13:37-38)?

7. What did the high priest quiz Jesus about? Why did Jesus resist giving extended answers to the questions? Why did the officer strike Jesus? How did Jesus's response highlight the illegality of this trial?

8. In what ways, both obvious and subtle, do you deny Christ? What situations make you susceptible to denying him?

9. Can you foresee a future situation in which you might be tempted to deny your Lord? What steps can you take now to plan to avoid it or form a different reaction?

SENTENCED TO DIE

JOHN 18:28–19:16

*P*ilate was a pitiful example of a man who was afraid of losing his position by doing the right thing. He was caught between his fear of offending the Jews and his fear of condemning an innocent man who claimed to be the Son of God. From our vantage point, it is easy to condemn Pilate's actions. But how often do we compromise what we know is right in order to save our own reputation or our position?

1. Have you ever been falsely accused of doing wrong? How did you react?

READ JOHN 18:28-40.

2. How was the hypocrisy of the Jewish leaders evidenced? What was faulty about the logic they used when accusing Jesus?

3. What adjectives describe Pilate's attitudes as he dealt with the Jewish leaders? with Jesus?

4. What do you think Pilate was trying to tell Jesus with his rhetorical question in verse 38?

5. Select adjectives to describe Jesus. Did he try to defend himself? Why or why not (verse 36)?

6. What insight into his mission did Jesus give?

7. What difficult or even desperate situations do you face? How does (or should) your relationship with God affect your response?

READ JOHN 19:1-16.

⤳ 8. Identify the different ways Jesus suffered or was humiliated. This suffering was predicted at various times in the Old Testament. What irony do you find in the Jewish religious leaders' fulfilling prophecy in this way?

9. Describe the stages of Pilate's struggle with his own conscience. What did he personally want to do? But what was more important to him?

∅ 10. What startling concession did the chief priests make (verse 15)? For them, why was it such a degrading compromise? What was their real motivation?

11. Was Jesus afraid of Pilate? Why or why not (verse 11)? How can Jesus's perspective help you face your own fears?

THE CROSS

JOHN 19:17-42

After Jesus's sham trial, he was brutally beaten and tortured. Then he was nailed to a cross. In addition to enduring the excruciating pain of crucifixion, the full weight of sin was placed upon him. Indeed, he became sin and felt the crushing wrath of God. He took the punishment for sin that humankind deserves. Why did he do it? So that anyone who believes in him can be reconciled to God and find eternal life.

1. When did the death of Christ begin to make sense to you?

READ JOHN 19:17-30.

2. How was the chief priests' continuing contempt for Jesus evidenced?

3. After it was too late, how did Pilate defend Jesus?

4. How was scriptural prophecy fulfilled during these events (verses 23-24,28-29)? (These events were prophesied in Psalms 22:18 and 69:21.) How do these prophecies help you understand Jesus's crucifixion more fully?

᷂ 5. What do you learn about Jesus from his last words on the cross (verses 26-28,30)?

READ JOHN 19:31-42.

6. How was the legalism of the Jews evidenced? What warped attitude toward pleasing God did this reveal?

7. What did John seem to be emphasizing about his gospel account in verse 35? What purpose did he have for writing it?

8. Describe the kinds of disciples that Joseph of Arimathea and Nicodemus were. What do their actions on Jesus's behalf indicate about their spiritual awareness?

9. In what ways are you a "secret disciple"? What opportunities might you have this week for being a "public disciple"?

10. How would you describe the necessity of the crucifixion of Christ to an unbelieving friend?

THE EMPTY TOMB

JOHN 20

The bodily resurrection of Jesus is one of the strongest facts about the Christian faith—yet for some, it's the most troubling. It is the one fact about Jesus that many people absolutely do not want to believe. Most people will admit he was a great moral teacher. Many admire him for being a non-violent, revolutionary leader. And just about everyone acknowledges the courage he displayed by dying a martyr's death. But people shy away from admitting that he rose from the dead. Why? Because that would strongly indicate that some of those other things were true—things like his being the Son of God and that faith in him alone is the only way to God.

1. Have you experienced periods of doubt in your life—times when faith in God seemed hard? What helped you through those times?

Read John 20:1-9.

2. When did Mary Magdalene arrive at the tomb? What does this indicate about her devotion to Jesus? What did she find?

3. What details about the empty tomb was John careful to report?

✎ 4. When the "other disciple" saw the empty tomb, he believed. Can you say when you first believed in Jesus? What prompted your belief?

Read John 20:10-23.

5. How did Mary react to the evidence at the tomb? What two events changed her feelings?

6. In what mood were the disciples and why? What happened to change their moods? What might you have thought and done if you had been in their shoes?

7. What act did Jesus perform here (verse 22)? What specific instructions did he give his disciples?

READ JOHN 20:24-31.

8. What do you already know about the way Thomas thought (see John 14:5)? What attitude did he adopt concerning Jesus's resurrection? Can you blame him?

9. What changed Thomas's mind? How do you know?

10. What encouragement can you take from Jesus's statement in verse 29? Why is it difficult to be one of those "who have not seen and yet have believed"? What resources do you have to overcome these difficulties (see John 14:25-26; 2 Timothy 3:16)?

11. What reason did John give for writing his gospel? How could you use what you know about this gospel to continue accomplishing John's original goal? To what key passages would you direct an honest seeker?

A CALL TO DISCIPLESHIP

JOHN 21

s you complete your final study in John's gospel, you face a great challenge. First, you need to decide what you believe about Jesus. After a fair examination of the historical facts in chapters 20 and 21, it might take more faith to disbelieve than to believe in Christ's resurrection. And yet, reason can take a person only so far. Proving a series of facts does not save a person. It takes personal faith in Jesus to gain eternal life. The second challenge is to follow Christ wholeheartedly. Look closely at this account of Jesus's breakfast with his disciples. Jesus challenged Peter, "Follow me"—even though he knew it would cost Peter his life. What about you? Will you follow Jesus whatever the cost?

1. Have you ever experienced failure to the extent you did not think you could be forgiven? What kinds of emotional obstacles did the experience put in your way?

READ JOHN 21:1-14.

2. What do you think Jesus was trying to emphasize to his disciples through this miracle?

3. How did Peter react to Jesus's seaside appearance? What insight does this give you into Peter's personality?

⤷ 4. Why do you think Jesus made breakfast for his disciples?

READ JOHN 21:15-25.

5. What might be the significance of Jesus's asking Peter three times if Peter loved him (see Luke 22:61-62)? How did Peter respond?

6. What do you think Jesus was referring to when he said, "Do you truly love me more than these?"

7. What command did Jesus emphasize to Peter? What did this mean for Peter? How does it apply to you?

8. Could Jesus's rebuke to Peter in verse 22 apply to you? When are you tempted to compare your situation or your degree of hardship with that of others?

9. What do you think Jesus was trying to teach Peter through the events in this passage—the miracle of the fish, the breakfast, and the three questions?

10. How does this account comfort you? How does it challenge you?

Leader's Notes

Study 1: The Living Word

Question 4. "God's attitude to all men is that of a Father. All are His sons in the sense that He made them and that He provides for them. But men are His sons in the full sense only as they respond to what He does for them in Christ. When they receive the Word they are born again (ch. 3) into the heavenly family. It is only in this way that they are God's *children*" (Leon Morris, *The Gospel According to John, The New International Commentary on the New Testament,* Grand Rapids: Eerdmans, 1983, p. 98).

Note on John 1:29-34. "As God had provided a lamb for sacrifice in the place of Isaac (Genesis 22:8), so Jesus is the Lamb provided by God to be sacrificed in the place of others. He also fulfills the ritual of the Passover in which the lamb was the effective symbol of salvation from destruction (see Exodus 12:3-17). Moreover, as a Lamb led to the slaughter and bearing the sins of many He discharges the role of the suffering Servant delineated in Isaiah 53. But John penetrates still deeper into the mystery of removing both its guilt and power" (R. V. G. Tasker, *The Gospel According to John,* Tyndale New Testament Commentaries, Grand Rapids: Eerdmans, 1971, p. 51).

Study 2: Come and See

Question 10. "The Jews demand a sign to authenticate His action and He gives them an answer which they misunderstand (cf. Mark 14:58). The temple, as the symbol of God's presence with His people, was theologically redundant, as the Word had become flesh and was tabernacling among men (1:14). It was doomed to destruction in due course, paradoxically through their possessive attitude to it.... But the new temple of Christ's body had to go through death to resurrection before it could be a spiritual temple and body of believers (1 Corinthians 3:16; 12:27)" (R. E. Nixon, *John,* Valley Forge, Pa.: Scripture Union, 1967, p. 11).

Study 3: New Life

Question 6. "Many people don't want their lives exposed to God's light because they are afraid of what it will reveal. They don't want to be changed. Don't be surprised when these same people are threatened by your desire to obey God and do what is right, because they are afraid that the light in you may expose some of the darkness in their lives" (*Life Application Bible,* Wheaton, Ill.: Tyndale, 1988, p. 1556).

Study 4: Living Water

Question 4. "What did Jesus mean by 'living water'? In the Old Testament, many verses speak of thirsting after God as one thirsts for water (Psalm 42:1; Isaiah 55:1; Jeremiah 2:13).... In saying he would bring living water that could forever quench one's thirst for God, Jesus was claiming to be the Messiah. Only the Messiah could give this free gift that satisfies the desire of the soul" (*Life Application Bible,* p. 1557).

Question 6. Spirit here does not mean Holy Spirit, although the Holy Spirit does assist our worship (Romans 8:27). Rather, Jesus is referring to our own spirits. True worship involves more than an outward observance. It must be a sincere response from the heart. *Truth* refers to the truth about Jesus's death and resurrection. Acceptance of this truth is now the necessary prerequisite to worshiping God.

Question 7. Jesus took time to converse with a woman most people shunned. He raised the questions about her past gently but firmly and challenged her to face the reality of her need. Jesus allowed the woman time to understand what he was talking about and to see the implications for her life.

Question 11. "The wages Jesus offers are the joy of working for him and seeing the harvest of believers. Usually a sower sees nothing but the seed, while the reaper sees the great reward of the harvest. But in Jesus' work, both will be rewarded by seeing new believers come into Christ's Kingdom. The phrase 'others have done the hard work' (4:38) could refer to the Old Testament prophets and/or John the Baptist" (*Life Application Bible,* p. 1559).

Study 5: Skepticism and Faith

Question 4. "The Pool of Bethesda was a shrine for sick people who wished to be healed and, presumably having despaired of a cure by other means, came in the superstitious hope that they might be able to benefit from the mysterious powers of the pool. Some manuscripts include verses 3b and 4 which state that an angel of the Lord went into the pool and troubled the water and the first person in after that was cured. This is no doubt simply a deduction from the authentic text and describes what was believed to happen" (Nixon, *John,* p. 21).

Question 8. Note the combination of humility and authority in Christ's character. He said he was like a son working in the family business, doing only what his father showed him. Yet he claimed that people must reverence him as they do God. If Jesus was merely a man, he was either crazy or infinitely proud to talk like this.

Question 9. John 5:29 talks about those who have done good and those who have done evil. "This does not mean that salvation is on the basis of good works, for this very Gospel makes it plain over and over again that men enter eternal life when they believe on Jesus Christ. But the lives they live form the test of the faith they profess. This is the uniform testimony of Scripture. Salvation is by grace and it is received through faith. Judgment is based on men's works" (Morris, *The Gospel According to John,* pp. 321-22).

Study 6: Bread of Life

Question 4. "They wanted to seize Him and proclaim Him a king. From this fate Jesus at once escaped by withdrawing to the hills to pray in solitude, for had He consented to their wish, He would have completely frustrated the purpose of His mission. He had not come primarily to satisfy men's material needs but their deep-seated, if not always recognized, need of forgiveness, without which they could not enjoy eternal life" (Tasker, *The Gospel According to John,* p. 93).

Question 13. Some people may be offended by Jesus's words, "eat my flesh and drink my blood." Calvin's commentary is helpful: "This confirms what was hard to believe—that souls feed on His flesh and blood in precisely the same way the body is sustained by eating and drinking" (John Calvin, *St. John, Calvin's New Testament Commentary,* Grand Rapids: Eerdmans, 1961, p. 169). John 6:63 indicates that Jesus did not mean for his words to be taken literally. "Eating and drinking" meant trusting in his life and death for salvation.

STUDY 7: WHO IS THIS JESUS?

Question 4. "The religious leaders had a great deal of power over the common people. It is apparent that they couldn't do much to Jesus at this time, but they threatened anyone who might publicly support him. Excommunication from the synagogue was one of the reprisals for believing in Jesus (9:22-23). To a Jew, this was one of the worst possible social stigmas" (*Life Application Bible,* p. 1567).

STUDY 8: SIN AND FORGIVENESS

Question 2. This passage is missing from most of the earliest Greek manuscripts of the gospel of John. Most later manuscripts include the verses at this point, though some insert them in other places. Most evangelical scholars agree with Dr. F. F. Bruce, who calls it "a fragment of authentic gospel material not originally included in any of the four Gospels" (F. F. Bruce, *The Gospel of John,* Grand Rapids: Eerdmans, 1983, p. 413).

Question 3. The law in Leviticus 20:10 called for both the man and the woman caught in adultery to be stoned. The Jewish leaders were displaying a double standard by bringing only the woman to Jesus.

Question 9. "*Lifted up the Son of man* (verse 28) is a curious expression, but it must point to the cross here as in other places where it occurs in the Gospel (3:14).... Jesus is saying that the Jews will not understand who he really is before they have crucified him" (Morris, *The Gospel According to John,* p. 452).

STUDY 9: GOD's TRUE CHILDREN

Question 6. Notice the way Jesus combined utter humility and complete assurance. When his enemies insulted him as strongly as they could, he was concerned only with what his Father thought of him (John 8:49-50). Yet he made confident claims about who he was and what he could do.

Question 8. "[John 8:58] is one of the most powerful statements uttered by Jesus. When he says he existed before Abraham was born, he undeniably proclaims his divinity.... Not only did Jesus say he existed before Abraham; he also applied God's holy name (I AM—Ex. 3:14) to himself. This claim demands a response. It cannot be ignored" (*Life Application Bible,* p. 1572).

STUDY 10: LIGHT IN THE DARKNESS

Question 2. "The disciples were bewildered by the seeming irrationality of an affliction which had befallen the man at birth, and which could not be traced to a definitive retributive judgment. They were more occupied in solving the abstract problem than in ministering to the individual that had aroused it. In short, they regarded him as a sinner who was less important than their debate" (Merrill C. Tenney, *John: The Gospel of Belief,* Grand Rapids: Eerdmans, 1948, p. 153).

Question 9. John 9:35-38 is a beautiful example of Jesus's compassion and concern for a bewildered, troubled person. Jesus took the initiative to look for him and to help him in his faith journey. The story ends with the healed man on his knees before Jesus. He has moved from unbelief to worship.

STUDY 11: THE GOOD SHEPHERD AND HIS SHEEP

Question 10. "A man who was merely a man and said the sort of things Jesus said would not be a great moral teacher. He would either be a lunatic—on level with a man who says he is a poached egg—or else he would be the Devil of Hell. You must make your choice. Either this man was, and is, the Son of God: or else a madman or something worse. You can shut Him up for a fool, you can spit at Him and kill Him for a demon; or you can fall at His feet and call Him Lord and God. But let us not come with any patronizing nonsense about His being a great moral teacher. He has not left that open to us. He did not intend to" (C. S. Lewis, *Mere Christianity*, New York: Macmillan, 1943, p. 56).

Study 12: Life and Death

Question 10. Jesus's prayer is a great example for us. His prayer was motivated by a desire for God's glory. He addressed God as his Father and prayed in faith. And his prayer was accompanied by thanksgiving to God for hearing him.

Study 13: Perfume and Praise

Question 8. "The principle in nature that death is essential for future life is applied by Jesus to Himself by inference. Wheat produces its own kind, and Jesus regards His passion in the same light. His death would bring many souls to life" (Donald Guthrie, *The New Bible Commentary, Revised: John,* Grand Rapids: Eerdmans, 1970, p. 956).

Study 14: The Last Supper

Question 9. "The glorification of Christ (John 13:31) is connected with what appears to men as the very opposite of glory. Jesus is looking to the cross as he speaks of glory. Origen employs the striking phrase, 'humble glory,' to express this idea of glory" (Morris, *The Gospel According to John,* p. 631).

Study 15: Comfort and Challenge

Question 7. "The continuity of revelation is guaranteed by the Holy Spirit. Because the disciples were human, they were likely to forget what Jesus said…. Even if [His words] were committed to writing immediately…false or inadequate interpretation could rob them of their true meaning. The voice of the Holy Spirit alone could stimulate the disciples' minds to recall the utterances of Jesus and could explain them correctly as needed" (Tenney, *John,* p. 224).

STUDY 16: VINES, BRANCHES, AND FRUIT

Question 3. "Many people try to do good, be honest, and do what is right. But Jesus says the only way to live a truly good life is to stay close to him, like a branch attached to the vine. Apart from him our efforts are unfruitful" (*Life Application Bible,* p. 1589).

Question 4. We may not be called upon to die for someone else, but there are other ways we can demonstrate sacrificial love by helping, encouraging, and giving.

Question 9. Since we are branches, we can draw life and strength from Jesus to do what is impossible on our own. Love and all the other fruit of the Spirit—joy, peace, patience, kindness, goodness, faithfulness, gentleness, and self-control—are possible because of his life flowing through us. In addition, he gives us the Holy Spirit to be our Comforter and the source of all truth.

STUDY 17: PEACE IN A TROUBLED WORLD

Question 7. In verse 16, Jesus was referring to his death and resurrection—events his disciples did not yet understand.

STUDY 18: JESUS'S FAREWELL PRAYER

Question 6. "Jesus didn't ask God to take believers out of the world but instead to use them in the world. Because Jesus sends us into the world, we should not try to escape from the world or avoid all relationships with non-Christians. We are called to be salt and light (Matthew 5:13-16), and we are to do the work God sent us to do" (*Life Application Bible,* p. 1592).

STUDY 19: ON TRIAL

Question 3. "It is possible that those in front recoiled from Jesus' unexpected advance, so they bumped those behind them, causing them to stumble and fall. But clearly what concerns John is the majesty of Jesus thus underlined" (Morris, *The Gospel According to John,* pp. 743-744).

Question 4. "In the Old Testament the 'cup' often has associations of suffering and of the wrath of God (Psalm 75:8; Isaiah 51:17; Jeremiah 25:15; Ezekiel 23:31-33). We cannot doubt that in this solemn moment these are the thoughts that the term arouses" (Morris, *The Gospel According to John,* p. 746).

STUDY 20: SENTENCED TO DIE

Question 2. "By Jewish law, entering the house of a Gentile would cause a Jewish person to be ceremonially defiled. As a result, he could not take part in worship at the Temple or feasts. Afraid of being defiled, these men stayed outside the home where they had taken Jesus for trial. They kept the pretenses of religion while harboring murder and treachery in their hearts" (*Life Application Bible,* p. 1596).

Question 8. Isaiah 53 is one example of Old Testament prophecy that predicted Jesus's suffering.

Question 10. The nation of Israel was founded on the kingship of God himself, which the people rejected when they demanded an earthly king (1 Samuel 8:7). The religious leaders were expressing the truth of their own spiritual condition when they said, "We have no king but Caesar." And they were denying any suggestion that they were rebels against Rome.

STUDY 21: THE CROSS

Question 5. John 19:26-27: It is possible that Jesus's brothers still did not believe in him, and Jesus was concerned for his mother's care. Verse 28: Death by crucifixion caused a burning thirst because of the fever that soon set in from the inflammation of wounds. Jesus also recognized the role of prophecy in his crucifixion. Verse 30: Jesus died victoriously, knowing he had accomplished all that God had given him to do. He voluntarily chose to give up his spirit in death.

Question 8. "Joseph of Arimathea was 'a rich disciple' (Matthew 27:57) and a member of the Sanhedrin who had not agreed to Jesus' condemnation (Luke 23:51).... It would have been hard for a member of the Sanhedrin to support Jesus' cause openly. Jesus' closest followers all ran away (Matthew 26:56), and it was left to Joseph and Nicodemus to provide for his burial" (*The NIV Study Bible,* Grand Rapids: Zondervan, 1985, p. 1635).

STUDY 22: THE EMPTY TOMB

Question 4. Regarding "the other disciple" in John 20:3,8: "Neither here nor elsewhere is this disciple named, but there seems no reason for doubting it was the apostle John.... Tradition unanimously supports John. No other name is suggested in antiquity" (Morris, *The Gospel According to John,* p. 625).

STUDY 23: A CALL TO DISCIPLESHIP

Question 4. In the Middle East, to eat a meal with someone who has wronged you is a way of expressing forgiveness. All of the disciples, not just Peter, were probably feeling terrible failure over their abandonment of Jesus at the time of his death. It was also important for the disciples to see Jesus eating as a normal human being. He was not just a ghost, but an actual person who had come back from death.

Question 6. "These" may refer to the fish and nets, symbols of Peter's profession, or to the other disciples. Peter had boasted that whatever others would do, he would never leave Jesus. Either way, Jesus's question is a rebuke.

What Should We Study Next?

*I*f you enjoyed this Fisherman Bible Studyguide, you might want to explore our full line of Fisherman Resources and Bible Studyguides. The following books offer time-tested Fisherman inductive Bible studies for individuals or groups.

FISHERMAN RESOURCES

The Art of Spiritual Listening: Responding to God's Voice Amid the Noise of Life by Alice Fryling

Balm in Gilead by Dudley Delffs

The Essential Bible Guide by Whitney T. Kuniholm

Questions from the God Who Needs No Answers: What Is He Really Asking of You? by Carolyn and Craig Williford

Reckless Faith: Living Passionately As Imperfect Christians by Jo Kadlecek

Soul Strength: Spiritual Courage for the Battles of Life by Pam Lau

FISHERMAN BIBLE STUDYGUIDES

Topical Studies

Angels by Vinita Hampton Wright

Becoming Women of Purpose by Ruth Haley Barton

Building Your House on the Lord: A Firm Foundation for Family Life (Revised Edition) by Steve and Dee Brestin

Discipleship: The Growing Christian's Lifestyle by James and
 Martha Reapsome
*Doing Justice, Showing Mercy: Christian Action in Today's
 World* by Vinita Hampton Wright
Encouraging Others: Biblical Models for Caring by Lin Johnson
The End Times: Discovering What the Bible Says by E. Michael
 Rusten
Examining the Claims of Jesus by Dee Brestin
Friendship: Portraits in God's Family Album by Steve and Dee
 Brestin
The Fruit of the Spirit: Cultivating Christlike Character by
 Stuart Briscoe
Great Doctrines of the Bible by Stephen Board
Great Passages of the Bible by Carol Plueddemann
Great Prayers of the Bible by Carol Plueddemann
Growing Through Life's Challenges by James and Martha
 Reapsome
Guidance & God's Will by Tom and Joan Stark
Heart Renewal: Finding Spiritual Refreshment by Ruth Goring
Higher Ground: Steps Toward Christian Maturity by Steve and
 Dee Brestin
Images of Redemption: God's Unfolding Plan Through the Bible
 by Ruth E. Van Reken
Integrity: Character from the Inside Out by Ted W. Engstrom
 and Robert C. Larson
Lifestyle Priorities by John White
Marriage: Learning from Couples in Scripture by R. Paul and
 Gail Stevens
Miracles by Robbie Castleman
One Body, One Spirit: Building Relationships in the Church by
 Dale and Sandy Larsen

The Parables of Jesus by Gladys Hunt

Parenting with Purpose and Grace: Wisdom for Responding to Your Child's Deepest Needs by Alice Fryling

Prayer: Discovering What Scripture Says by Timothy Jones and Jill Zook-Jones

The Prophets: God's Truth Tellers by Vinita Hampton Wright

Proverbs and Parables: God's Wisdom for Living by Dee Brestin

Satisfying Work: Christian Living from Nine to Five by R. Paul Stevens and Gerry Schoberg

Senior Saints: Growing Older in God's Family by James and Martha Reapsome

The Sermon on the Mount: The God Who Understands Me by Gladys M. Hunt

Speaking Wisely: Exploring the Power of Words by Poppy Smith

Spiritual Disciplines: The Tasks of a Joyful Life by Larry Sibley

Spiritual Gifts by Karen Dockrey

Spiritual Hunger: Filling Your Deepest Longings by Jim and Carol Plueddemann

A Spiritual Legacy: Faith for the Next Generation by Chuck and Winnie Christensen

Spiritual Warfare: Disarming the Enemy Through the Power of God by A. Scott Moreau

The Ten Commandments: God's Rules for Living by Stuart Briscoe

Ultimate Hope for Changing Times by Dale and Sandy Larsen

When Faith Is All You Have: A Study of Hebrews 11 by Ruth E. Van Reken

Where Your Treasure Is: What the Bible Says About Money by James and Martha Reapsome

Who Is God? by David P. Seemuth

Who Is Jesus? In His Own Words by Ruth E. Van Reken

Who Is the Holy Spirit? by Barbara H. Knuckles and Ruth E. Van Reken

Wisdom for Today's Woman: Insights from Esther by Poppy Smith

Witnesses to All the World: God's Heart for the Nations by Jim and Carol Plueddemann

Women at Midlife: Embracing the Challenges by Jeanie Miley

Worship: Discovering What Scripture Says by Larry Sibley

Bible Book Studies

Genesis: Walking with God by Margaret Fromer and Sharrel Keyes

Exodus: God Our Deliverer by Dale and Sandy Larsen

Ruth: Relationships That Bring Life by Ruth Haley Barton

Ezra and Nehemiah: A Time to Rebuild by James Reapsome

(For Esther, see Topical Studies, *Wisdom for Today's Woman*)

Job: Trusting Through Trials by Ron Klug

Psalms: A Guide to Prayer and Praise by Ron Klug

Proverbs: Wisdom That Works by Vinita Hampton Wright

Ecclesiastes: A Time for Everything by Stephen Board

Song of Songs: A Dialogue of Intimacy by James Reapsome

Jeremiah: The Man and His Message by James Reapsome

Jonah, Habakkuk, and Malachi: Living Responsibly by Margaret Fromer and Sharrel Keyes

Matthew: People of the Kingdom by Larry Sibley

Mark: God in Action by Chuck and Winnie Christensen

Luke: Following Jesus by Sharrel Keyes

John: An Eyewitness Account of the Son of God by Whitney T. Kuniholm

Acts 1–12: God Moves in the Early Church by Chuck and Winnie Christensen

Acts 13–28, see *Paul* under Character Studies
Romans: The Christian Story by James Reapsome
1 Corinthians: Problems and Solutions in a Growing Church by
    Charles and Ann Hummel
Strengthened to Serve: 2 Corinthians by Jim and Carol
    Plueddemann
Galatians, Titus, and Philemon. Freedom in Christ by Whitney
    Kuniholm
Ephesians: Living in God's Household by Robert Baylis
Philippians: God's Guide to Joy by Ron Klug
Colossians: Focus on Christ by Luci Shaw
Letters to the Thessalonians by Margaret Fromer and Sharrel
    Keyes
Letters to Timothy: Discipleship in Action by Margaret Fromer
    and Sharrel Keyes
Hebrews: Foundations for Faith by Gladys Hunt
James: Faith in Action by Chuck and Winnie Christensen
1 and 2 Peter, Jude: Called for a Purpose by Steve and Dee
    Brestin
1, 2, 3 John: How Should a Christian Live? by Dee Brestin
Revelation: The Lamb Who Is the Lion by Gladys Hunt

Bible Character Studies
Abraham: Model of Faith by James Reapsome
David: Man After God's Own Heart by Robbie Castleman
Elijah: Obedience in a Threatening World by Robbie
    Castleman
Great People of the Bible by Carol Plueddemann
King David: Trusting God for a Lifetime by Robbie Castleman
Men Like Us: Ordinary Men, Extraordinary God by Paul
    Heidebrecht and Ted Scheuermann

Moses: Encountering God by Greg Asimakoupoulos

Paul: Thirteenth Apostle (Acts 13–28) by Chuck and Winnie
   Christensen

Women Like Us: Wisdom for Today's Issues by Ruth Haley
   Barton

Women Who Achieved for God by Winnie Christensen

Women Who Believed God by Winnie Christensen